CountryMusic ★ Stars
KENNY CHESNEY

By Rene Wilson

Gareth Stevens
Publishing

RIGHT ON!

Please visit our Web site www.garethstevens.com. For a free color catalog of all our high-quality books, call toll free 1-800-542-2595 or fax 1-877-542-2596.

Library of Congress Cataloging-in-Publication Data

Wilson, Rene.
  Kenny Chesney / Rene Wilson.
       p. cm. — (Country music stars)
  Includes index.
  ISBN 978-1-4339-3608-1 (pbk.)
  ISBN 978-1-4339-3609-8 (6-pack)
  ISBN 978-1-4339-3607-4 (library binding)
  1. Chesney, Kenny—Juvenile literature. 2. Country musicians—United States—
Biography—Juvenile literature. I. Title.
  ML3930.C448W55 2010
  782.421642092—dc22
  [B]
                                        2009037568

Published in 2010 by Gareth Stevens Publishing
111 East 14th Street, Suite 349
New York, NY 10003

Copyright © 2010 Gareth Stevens Publishing

Designer: Haley Harasymiw
Editor: Mary Ann Hoffman

Photo credits: Cover (background), pp. 17, 19 Shutterstock.com; cover, p. 1(Kenny Chesney) © Bryan Bedder/Getty Images; p. 5 © Chris Weeks/Getty Images; p. 7 © Michael Loccisano/Getty Images; pp. 9, 11 © Tim Mosenfelder/Getty Images; pp. 13, 15 © Ethan Miller/Getty Images; p. 21 © Beth Gwinn/Redferns/Getty Images; pp. 23, 29 © Scott Gries/Getty Images; p. 25 © Ray Tamarra/Getty Images; p. 27 © Austin K. Swift/Getty Images.

Printed in the United States of America

CPSIA compliance information: Batch #CW10GS: For further information contact Gareth Stevens, New York, New York at 1-800-542-2595.

CONTENTS

A BORN STAR

Kenny Chesney writes, sings, and plays country music. He was born on March 26, 1968.

Kenny grew up in Knoxville, Tennessee. As a young boy, Kenny liked to listen to all kinds of music.

A SPECIAL GIFT

Kenny got a guitar as a gift when he was 19. He taught himself to play it.

IN A BAND

Kenny became a very good guitar
player. He joined a band in college.

A SONGWRITER

Kenny began to write songs. He played his songs for people.

Kenny worked very hard to earn money. He played and sang in many different cities.

RECORDING HIS MUSIC

In 1989, Kenny recorded some of his

music. He sold about 1,000 copies.

NASHVILLE

In 1991, Kenny moved to Nashville, Tennessee. He kept writing, playing, and singing his music.

Kenny's first album came out in 1994.

He has recorded many other albums.

Many people buy his music.

21

Kenny has won many music awards.

He has won awards for videos, too!

HIS FANS

Kenny has many fans. He takes time
to meet them.

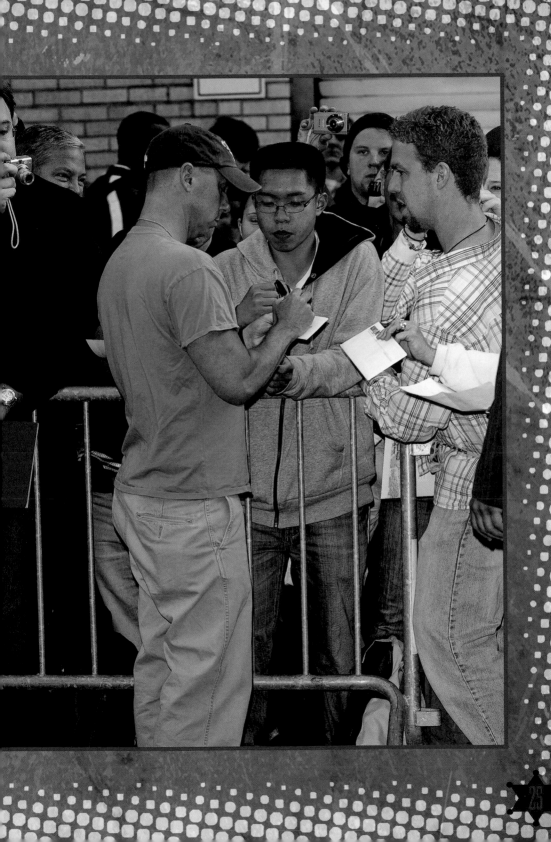

Kenny sings and plays with other country stars. Here, he is singing with Taylor Swift.

ENTERTAINER OF THE YEAR!

Kenny has been named Entertainer of the Year many times!

29

TIMELINE

1968   Kenny is born in Knoxville, Tennessee.

1989   Kenny first records his songs.

1991   Kenny moves to Nashville, Tennessee.

1994   Kenny's first album comes out.

2002   Kenny wins his first music video award.

2004   Kenny wins his first award for Entertainer of the Year.

FOR MORE INFORMATION

Books:

Adams, Michele Medlock. *Kenny Chesney*. Hockessin, DE: Mitchell Lane Publishers, 2007.

Thomas, William David. *Kenny Chesney*. Milwaukee, WI: Gareth Stevens Publishing, 2008.

Thomson, Cindy. *Kenny Chesney*. Broomall, PA: Mason Crest, 2009.

Web Sites:

CMT: Kenny Chesney

www.cmt.com/artists/az/chesney_kenny/artist.jhtml

Kenny Chesney

www.kennychesney.com/home.php

GLOSSARY

album: a collection of recorded music

award: a prize given to someone for doing something well

college: a school after high school

entertainer: a person who acts, sings, dances, or plays music for other people

guitar: a musical instrument with a flat body, long neck, and strings

record: to copy musical sound so that it can be listened to over and over

video: a short movie that goes along with a song

INDEX